INCOGNITUM

INCOGNITUM

AUBRIE MARRIN

First published in the United Kingdom in 2015 by
Shearsman Books
50 Westons Hill Drive
Emersons Green
BRISTOL
BS16 7DF

Shearsman Books Ltd Registered Office
30–31 St. James Place, Mangotsfield, Bristol BS16 9JB
(this address not for correspondence)

www.shearsman.com

ISBN 978-1-84861-397-3

Cover art © 2003 by George Boorujy
Brandt's Cormorant, ink on paper, 96"x40"

for Ryan Murphy

TABLE OF CONTENTS

...I'd have
nightmares of other islands
stretching away from mine, infinities
of islands, islands spawning islands....
....knowing that I had to live
on each and every one, eventually,
for ages, registering their flora,
their fauna, their geography.

—*Elizabeth Bishop, "Crusoe in England"*

HALF-LIFE

The maple tree in the yard
halved from lightning,

bare hills saddled with
houses, hives

of development and the scourge
of bulldozed ground.

There are the new strip malls,
the polluted creek,

the paper pulp mill
up in flames.

Ignited suburban night,
nightgown clouds

for plumage, shadows
without shirts.

It's all part of you
and then—

I don't mean
to disturb you.

These are the seven days
of clouds.

These are the ten days
of clouds.

The middle of June,
we take in

the hydrangeas because
of frost.

I am speaking plainly here.

The screen doors changed
to storm doors.

The peach tree lost
to infestation,

fruitless and weepy
with golden sap.

The tranquilizers,

    little white
    seeds—

they aren't working.

AMERICA

Parking lots laid with smoking asphalt
in the night.

Did I tell you I was Little Miss Hudson Valley?

Meltwater, dumped sediment, a glacier's
groove, what's left behind.

The last great boneyard disappears
behind the sign

WE KNOW EVERY MOVE YOU MAKE
ARNOFF MOVING & SELF-STORAGE

The opossums have secret meetings
in the trees.

Flashbulbs pop, they lift the plastered cast
of the Mastodon from the marl pit
for the first time in Newburgh, New York.

O eighteenth century
American Monster,

O Incognitum.

Did I tell you my dress was white
and I rode in the parade?

All night watchmen drive around
car auction lots big as Texas.

Blinking lights. Stop & Shop.
We're here.

AVICULARIA, 1705, FROM *METAMORPHOSIS INSECTORUM SURINAMENSIUM*

To see, expertly, how things
change—

> *chrysalises and so on.*

Branch of guava tree with ants,
spiders, and hummingbird.

Or more specifically—

> Tarantula on top,
> hummingbird supine
> and envenomated.

I apologize in advance
for the birds,

> I do not use them
> recklessly.

I don't apologize
for the clutch of spiders.

Oh those articulated
legs.

> Every piece of the machine
> at war with another.

This isn't the meaning
I intended.

Or more precisely—

you the predatory

            star.

THE ANATOMY OF MELANCHOLY

The climate's changed.

Nothing grows
quite so big as before.

What it is: With all the Kinds, Causes, Symptomes,
Prognostickes, and Several Cures of it.

        Philosophically, Medicinally, Historically,

        Opened and Cut Up.

That's just the subtitle.

        This is the heart
        that seeks

        and finds
        the flaw.

The prehistoric anteater
walks the hospital grounds,

the magnolia trees
so much smaller now.

Everything's repeated.

The catbirds collect
our discarded hair.

        Once this was a shallow inland sea.

        Once there was a center.

THE NATURALIST, 1855

In New Guinea
you will need provisions:

    fifteen pounds gunpowder,
    four thousand percussion caps
    and bags of bullets,

    ten pounds arsenic and other
    preservatives,

    two narrow cases for bird skins,
    ten boxes for storing insects

    and six thousand
    insect pins.

With the pigeons, the thing is

        to skeletonise them
        & watch their insides.

You might think the jungle's
a rhythmic wooded landscape,
the whole place simply

made of trees and how they are
moving, and in moving
disappearing.

The expedition could fail,

        Alfred Russell Wallace holed up
        during the monsoon in a Sarawak river
        shack on Borneo's North coast.

I want to carve
a hole in the hardwood

just big enough
for my body—

> *Terrible wet weather...*
> *nothing to eat & all of us ill.*

Stuck on the continent

without
a language,

arsenic and
sawdust sleep—

but still, months or maybe weeks later,
capturing the Ornithoptera,

> *the largest, the most perfect,*
> *and the most beautiful of butterflies,*
>
> *its golden body & crimson breast.*

POSTCARD TO MILLBROOK, I

Dear

    I'm sounding things
    out—

    acan aken ache
    ahr kee OP tuhr ihks.

        George Stubbs was obsessed
        with painting white mares
        in the moment of being
        attacked by lions.

What's going to happen
to the slow lorises
in the Millbrook zoo?

    Osama Bin Laden is dead.

I pledge allegiance
to my dark

    botig botah body,

to the Oldsmobile sleeping now
on the frozen river.

WISDOM OF GOD MANIFESTED IN
THE WORKS OF HIS CREATION

Don't worry, I've killed
the last snake

that lived in the wood shed,
coiled copperhead.

In these parts
everything points toward

                    yes.

Peeling billboards
along the highway.

Abandoned colonials,
tinder of sunken porches.

To want so badly
to be lit.

            Thomas Jefferson writes to his friend,
            General George Rogers Clark—

                        *No matter about the Indians
                        at Big Bone Lick, Kentucky,
                        just bring me all the bones
                        you can find.*

Our bones are bigger
than your bones.

Incognita—

word is
I am a

good girl.

This bird, little
bomb, pretty bomb,

colored insides,
blinking lights—

singing *firecracker firecracker
tick tick boom,*

singing smoke and sulfur—

set it in the crook
of the tulip tree.

Put it back where
it came from.

MAD MAUDLIN'S SEARCH FOR HER TOM OF BEDLAM

The search over the flat lake
stagnant with pondweed,

pickerelweed, dollar bonnet,
maidencane, spatterdock.

There's no compass here.

The toothy dredge crackles
along the bottom,

uprooting snails
and snappers.

> *Put your foot in that water,*
> *and you'll lose a toe,*
> *or worse, a whole foot.*

Creaturely body,
scummed over, skimmed by

the herons and egrets,
and with nowhere to go.

He's talking
to himself again.

I'm the woman on the plane reading
Codex on the Flight of Birds.

Drag and lift,
yaw and pitch,

get me out
of here.

Heartsick has a smell,
a blue smell,

a country rain
on a stagnant lake,

sulphurous mud,
pinpricks on the water,

blooms of algae
green as bile.

He can hear me,
tinny sparrow
in a mildewed ear.

Even without a map

it's chip and cheep—
it's sing.

ARCHAEOPTERYX, THE BERLIN SPECIMEN, 1874

At the most what's left
behind is an outline—

> death-pose, feathers pressed
> into a white lake
> of limestone.

So something gathers around
the body,

and you the first with a complete
head, however

> crushed.

Room of tar, seeping petroleum pit
of sedative sleep—

> I appear in the yard
> I ward off deer, I scatter
> my hair in the garden.

O Klonopin, golden tokens
for the broken,

> in the room of no sleep
> teach me to make
> house.

Held up by hooks under
the armpits, I'm still

alive, I'm missing
a tooth, I've lost

all my animal
shape.

The emotional center inevitably shifts—
depth charge

        in a quarry lake,
        some quake,

sharp pixel of light in the gut
browning out.

POSTCARD TO MILLBROOK, II

Dear

    Animal bones
    pressed in city
    asphalt.

I'm talking about
being human.

I'll never be a real
home owner.

    In the isolation room
    you coughed and coughed
    your way

        out of here.

I hear the loons out
on your lake sounding out
the sounds

lunaticus, lunatic

    see the luna moth
    clinging to the screen.

KOLOMBANGARA

I want the words
to mean something.

In the cloud forests
of Kolombangara
there's all sorts of babble,

everyone's talking,

       they all drown
       each other out.

Giant laughingthrush, rufous-rumped
grassbird, flame-templed
babbler, splendid white-eye.

Days are days,
various shades of white
on white grey on white
grey on grey.

Nothing distinguishable.

Interglacial.

I'm afraid of Southwest
mega-droughts,

       other unnameable
       things.

If the birds have white feathers
rimming their eyes,

they call them
white-eyes.

Please repeat after me—

        I shall not want,
        I don't want

    I can't place
    your name.

SEABIRDS

The albatross
slope soaring

over the Atlantic,
surface seizing

         prey,

breeding and dancing,
sky-pointing—

Have you ever seen
a hurricane?

Your harnessed body
scales the mast,

       goes down into
       the engine room
       chest deep in bilge
       water—

The water
rises.

I keep these facsimiles
for myself.

O of my mouth,
birds up my sleeves—

these are the only
magic tricks

I have left.

HERCULANEUM

The whole of it is collapsing—
first the colors

go, and then the sound. If you leave
the back door

unlatched at night I draw raccoons
right into the house,

        it's true.

Dark houses, a dark rocking
chamber, a hand

at the end
of a rope.

The last hours have always been here,
secret things—

a stilled, pyroclastic flow behind
the eyes,

the moments before the car,
left in neutral,

rolls down
the hill.

The eruption—a burning cloud
pushing even the sea back.

Bodies, years later, perfectly preserved
on the beach.

According to the letters of Pliny the Younger,
the cloud

was like a Mediterranean pine
more than any other tree,

a very high tree,

        expanding into
        infinite branches.

DISCOURSE ON THE REVOLUTIONARY UPHEAVALS ON THE SURFACE OF THE GLOBE AND ON THE CHANGES THEY PRODUCED IN THE ANIMAL KINGDOM

The animals are awake now.
I wear bells on my wrists
and ankles so as not to

      take the lions by surprise.

Can you see me
through the trees?

Supermoon, yes, I am
troubled.

      It wasn't until the end of the 18th century
      that French paleontologist and anatomist
      Georges Cuvier demonstrated incontrovertible
      proof that extinction was real.

      Extinctions,
      plural.

First proof of these upheavals—

Then proof that these revolutions
have been numerous—

Then proof that these revolutions
have been sudden.

Birds of America,

      Chrysalis—this
      is extinction,

cloud-dump, grey houses, grey roads.
Something always decomposing
into something else.

Keys made here.

The animals know something
we don't.

Toolool toolool
wheedlee wheedlee

I can't move
my mouth

like that.

Maybe it's a kind of
talking but I want to believe
it isn't talking at all.

I want to interrupt
myself over and over.

Audubon regularly burned
first drafts to force continuous
improvement.

There aren't any
distinguishable markings
and I don't want
to scare you

but I am
devoted.

Bioluminescent.

Swamp pink in the seascapes,
islands being born—

they're not enough, these bare
nouns.

       A shoal of bass, sleuth of bears,
       sedge of bitterns, a deceit

              of lapwings—

I'm learning.

     I'll whisper
     catastrophe in your ear.

SIN NOMBRE VIRUS

The deer mice are taking over
the forests in Durango,

the Aspen trees
are in a sudden
decline.

At night I say *Svalbard*
in my sleep,

I dream of the Global Seed Vault,
cache after cache of heat-sealed
four-ply seed pouches,

> Claytonia Miner's Lettuce,
> some rare heifer,

> a full head of
> human hair.

The secrets a pelvic bone
tells,

how whale bones poke through
the beach sand.

Willow, Alder, a sucking wound—

I know a sickness—
I know it knows me,

but I don't know
how the bones
will be scattered.

STILL LIFE

Fashion a diving cormorant
to the wall

      so that it looks like it's flying.

      How to—

I haven't taken very good care
of my skin,

      I'm sorry.

The body gives off
light

and the body gives off
darkness.

      If the weather should be warm,
      be pleased to order the Bowels
      to be taken out and some Pepper
      put into the Body, but no salt
      which would spoil the feathers.

Knowing in the beginning
that there is an ending.

Removing meat from the skin—

they call this phase
fleshing.

Take this spoon
to my skull

with pathological
fidelity.

I won't be the same shape,

       I will lose my eyes,

and anyway it's not going
to work,

       I'm not
       aerodynamic—

but I want to be   still   and

handcrafted.

CALENTURE

Who do you think you are,
with all these birds in your bag,
some kind of Leatherstocking?

Do not touch the birds,
they are covered in arsenic poison.

I am Trapper, I am Pathfinder, I am Deerslayer.

Come into my diorama. Everything's life size.
Everything's as it should be in the wild.

You've got no business with
the grotesque, with arsenical soap,
with any kind of preservation.

Taxidermy is just Greek
for the arrangement of skin,

        the magical business
        of putting things back together
        bone by bone.

See me cocking my head
to the side?

No setting the switch
of the heart back.

Where the sailors think the sea
a grassy green field and just step in—

This is make-believe.

I have no drug
save this one.

A NATURALIST IN A CANNIBAL LAND, 1903

In the New Guinea swamps,
the fever,

     and the outbreaks of measles
     in the villages.

Sugaring trees by day
with treacle, beer,
and pears,

     luring moths
     big as a hand
     by lamp light—

You know something
of transformation.

Carrying killing-bottles
with cyanide of potassium
for killing small insects

and syringes with acetic acid
for killing the large,

     you are no navigator,
     have no compass.

You don't stop.

You bring your tobacco
and iron roofs.

The great pupa
of loss

stirs in its jar.

Inside, your blood
pulses with malaria,

body shivering
and sweating—

A.S. Meek swimming
in a plasmodium dream.

*I have heard that when a crocodile
captures a calf or a human being,
it is usual for it to hide away the body
for some days before devouring it.*

The Birds of Paradise
have no feet—

this kind of
transformation.

For who ever really wanted
the kingdom of God
on earth anyway.

NUMBERS

Partially digested
human jaw bone

pulled from the stomach
of an alligator.

      Can I count on you?

Coded messages, blinking
icons, news feeds.

The house emptied
for auction, light

        spilling in,

the mattress slumped
on the floor.

      Goodness

        three hearts can't be
        better than one—

I'm counting to ten.

The dirt gets tossed
on top.

The songbirds, the baby
pigeon,

everything just dies
in my hands.

POSTCARD TO MILLBROOK, III

Dear

My x-ray, luminous
black and white
on the light board

      while outside goldenrod
      bursts from the roadside
      and waste places
      with jaundiced eyes,

   Solidago Canadensis.

   O Canada,

      the complicated body.

Yellow, yellow, yellow

      They clearcut the forest
      like grief gone through
      the heart.

In our own way,

each of us
is the most

      dangerous person
      to have ever lived.

LORD KING GOD BIRD

Even as
the whole of it
is eaten by beetles

I don't have
eyes for

I don't want

I say out loud

    rescue me
    from the mouth
    of the lions.

Pearly Bill,

your raised red crest
nowhere in the Sweet Gums,

 gone in Arkansas' Prairie Lakes,
 in the Tupelo and Bald Cypresses,
 the Oaks and Hickories—

Faulkner's Big Woods.

I have a gypsy moth in a jar,
splinters from a telephone poll.

    Do the preserved still poison
    their preservers?

It all gathers, it comes like
a wrecking ball

     to the light
     of seven o'clock.

YUCCA MOUNTAIN

The telephone's ringing
all the time.

If you look at the seamless image
that is the world

the Mojave desert is to your right,
the Great Basin desert to your left.

You are in this picture.

You are holding it all together
and the fog, the whiteout of fog

over Gowanus is paperweight
to terror.

The transplants in the garden
take.

We have no long-term storage plans
for nuclear waste.

It's all dandelions and lawn slugs
in the heart.

I point to places where
you should grow.

THE IVORY-BILLED WOODPECKER
PLATE CCLVI, FROM *BIRDS OF AMERICA*

Meaningless particles
of disintegration

      I want to report
      a sighting.

What are the known
 sounds.

What is the harmonic
interval.

Three foot wingspan over
the purple loosestrife,

      above road sludge
      and wrecked heron nests,

      over piles of Goodyear tires
      thrown like lifesavers—

How many pills
does one girl need.

          They sometimes cling to the bark
          with their claws so firmly, as to remain
          cramped to the spot for several hours
          after death.

Did you talk any differently
at the end?

Did you sing?

The insects are so loud
clicking their hearts
in the dark.

Lord King God Bird
I think I am the one

        being studiously
        dissected.

BOWER BIRD

There's beautiful
danger here—

holus-bolus hovel,
dollhouse done up

>
> with dull shards of glass,
> blanched sheep vertebrae,
>
> bottle caps,
> rifle shell casings,
>
> pebbles and piles of nuts,
> dead beetles,
>
> garlands strung
> with caterpillar feces.

This all tastes
blue.

Some damp leaves,
sprays of fern dotted

with aphid eggs
on their undersides,

>
> handfuls of your hair,
> a blue-footed mushroom.

Song and dance,
a short bout of mimicry—

> that's not what
> I mean.

Talk to me like a waterfall.

King of nothing,
blow the house
down.

> Did I tell you I can put both legs
> behind my head?

I'll lie face down
in the underbrush,

> you just get on top of me.

PLASMA AND POISON

However mangrove
the mouth

of the bays   I don't have

the radial symmetry
of a flower

or these lion's mane
jellyfish, so much more

      than plasma
      or poison—

tentacles trailing
one hundred feet
or more behind,

      translucent
      bridal trains.

There is a space in the left lung
where the heart fits,

      cardiac notch—

and lungs are just

      new & improved
      swim bladders.

Tinseled shoals,
undertow ghost—

I am home

in the snow
of whale fall

      coming down.

I passive floater,
we weak thing,

      us seeping
      and anoxic.

It's important to say
I am alive.

DINOSAUR HEART

Of the heart, of what cannot
be qualified.

Grapefruit-sized,
a brown reddish clump

sleeping for sixty-six million years
in South Dakotan sandstone,

maybe in the outcrop of rock
the four chambers

               beat on and on—

Of the heart, its single systemic aorta
lies exposed in the chest,

a clump of stone.

Of course there's more
to say—

          skull caved in,
          spinal column clearly

          visible,

ribs showing like blunt knives—

               Erosion.

Thescelosaurus neglectus,

on and on,
down through

the wormhole geologic
and volatile—

feathers and scales glinting
with the heredity

    of despair.

Marvelous, neglected—

    we're smaller now.

SPECIMEN DAYS

The stupor passes, something else
begins.

The blue everywhere, ambulance
processions,

birds migrating at midnight—
the bobolink is there, the tanager—

birds and birds and birds.
Birds—and a caution.

        This isn't some sort of scrapbook,
        you know.

        The bodies don't get dropped
        here.

I turn South—and then East again
along America's back-bone.

Convulsiveness. The great unrest
of which we are part

and Walt says the real war will never
get in the books.

The weather—does it sympathize
with these times.

What kind of specimen
are you.

What will you do with your
electric body, its mouth.

      The thyroid is shaped like a butterfly,
      remove it with a knife

      and pin it to the bedroom wall, pretend
      it isn't over yet.

LAZARUS TAXA

This difficulty. Talking to the one
who isn't there,

the aurochs, light eel stripe
along the back,

head of massive horns. Who do you
really know

anyway. The grasslands open.
After a period

of apparent absence you reappear.
Talk to me I am

in the other room. Difficult
to explain.

The particular quality of light then.
Does the body

look any different. The hide.
I'm looking

for various kinds of time, space
time, deep

time. The aurochs moves like I imagine
it would,

the stride, the muscles, etc. I'm a difficult
person.

Whoever you are, I ask to be
gored through the thigh.

Anything to bring us back
singing.

DIORAMA WITH RICHARD OWEN

Terrible + powerful + wondrous,

      ambiguous modes
      of expression

      and his
      Dinosauria,

so life-like—

    natural history
    his dancing bear.

He laid the dead rhinoceros
in the hallway.

Days later, from the diary
of his wife, Caroline:

      R. still at the rhinoceros.

Tell me about the mysteries
of vertebrates,

to wake up and see
order, a system

      a web of mutual
      dependencies?

MASTODON DREAM

Your tusks are breaking branches.

You march through marsh
all skeleton, articulated body

bare white in the swamp
the airport made.

The herons have left.

We're alone.

When they found you in our bog
you stood exactly as you'd died—

massive body upright, legs thrust forward,
head tilted upward and gasping for air.

What mattered most to us
was your head.

> *I regret very much the loss of this head,*
> *it is impossible to save those that are taken*
> *out of the water, and it is in the water or*
> *Mires the Most entire bones are found.*

Your skeletal trunk wraps round
my waist.

We're family.

Nipple-tooth teeth, tusks a ton each,
swagger and stomp

through the Super 8 parking lot,
past the sleeping big rigs

and diesel tanks, up the entry ramp
to the highway.

My skinned and de-fleshed Lovely,
my Dearest Pet,

in the fluorescent flood-lit night
we're undiscovered,

bone-white and weightless.

POSTCARD TO MILLBROOK, IV

Dear

Hurricane Mountain, Paradox Lake,
Spectator—

        these places
        are for real.

Snoqualmie is just
an old Lushootseed word
meaning

        ferocious people.

Sumac bobs god-smacked red
magnolia blossoms opened
past opening—

    I love you crab grass,

    I love you sprawling empty lots—

        During his honeymoon, George Stubbs
        stayed in a two-room cottage, in one room
        hanging up the decaying carcass of a horse
        that he lovingly dissected.

    Junebug, here I
    pin your eyes.

THE VIVIPAROUS QUADRUPEDS OF NORTH AMERICA

Mammal to mammal,

    I don't know if there's a protagonist
    in this story. We may or may not be
    responsible for each other's happiness.

        Eutheria,
        from the Greek

for true good beasts.

I say your name out loud
like it's a latinate,

like it matters.

    I dead float in the community pool.

        My bones say
        please remember me.

ODE

The couple found weighted
down in Wiley's pond—

blue lips, blue heels, their arms
flailing now, their ankles

      breaking free.

They're waving to you
like old friends.

Dredging the pond
for hours

eluding hooks they do
their slow underwater waltz.

I say out loud

      I am afraid.

The bindings dissolving
from rot,

      ankles breaking free.

Something knows
what's lost—

sound of dry leaves
under the rusted car,

        sagging creek bridge.

With the woodpiles
and the new generator,

the house won't go
cold without you.

The day you hid in the closet
at four, it disowned you.

Hair-pin turns, dirt roads,
slabs of glacier-dropped granite—

you sunned on those rocks,
chalked your name on those rocks,

        even when the sky
        turned against you.

The Hudson Valley, draped
discarded scar.

The houses come at you
from all sides.

        Where do you think
        you're going?

NOTES

"American Monster" and "American Incognitum" were some of the names given to the fossilized skeletons of the Mastodons found in the United States in the late eighteenth century.

The title "Avicularia, 1705, from *Metamorphosis Insectorum Surinamensium*" is taken from a plate by naturalist and scientific illustrator Maria Sibylla Merian, from her book *Metamorphosis Insectorum Surinamensium*, or *Metamorphosis of the Insects of Surinam*.

The phrase "chrysalises and so on" is taken from the forward to Merian's *Metamorphosis of the Insects of Surinam*.

The Anatomy of Melancholy—What it is: With all the Kinds, Causes, Symptomes, Prognostickes, and Several Cures of it. In Three Maine Partitions with their several Sections, Members, and Subsections. Philosophically, Medicinally, Historically, Opened and Cut Up is a book by Robert Burton published in 1621.

The line "to skeletonise them / & watch their insides" is taken from the notebooks Charles Darwin kept during his studies of pigeons.

The lines "Terrible wet weather... / nothing to eat & all of us ill" and "the largest, the most perfect, / and the most beautiful of butterflies / its golden body & crimson breast" are taken from the diary of Alfred Russel Wallace, a British naturalist, explorer, and biologist.

George Stubbs was an English painter, best known for his paintings of horses. In 1756 he rented a farmhouse in the village of

Horkstow, Lincolnshire, and spent eighteen months dissecting horses, assisted by his common-law wife, Mary Spencer.

Wisdom of God Manifested in the Works of His Creation is the title of a book by British naturalist John Ray, published in 1691.

The lines "No matter about the Indians / at Big Bone Lick, Kentucky, / just bring me all the bones / you can find" are inspired by Thomas Jefferson's letters to General George Rogers Clark and William Clark, in his efforts to recover a full American Incognitum, or American Mastodon, skeleton in order to disprove the theory of American Degeneracy put forward by French naturalist George Louis Leclerc, Comte de Buffon, stating that the animals of the New World, including the United States, lacked the size, vigor, and variety of European animals.

"Mad Maudlin's Search for Her Tom of Bedlam" was a popular ballad poem based on "Tom O'Bedlam," an anonymous poem written circa 1600 about bedlamites, the former inmates of the Bethlem Royal Hospital in London for the mentally ill.

The Archaeopteryx is a genus of early bird considered a transitional species between feathered dinosaurs and modern birds. The Berlin Specimen is the name for a specific Archaeopteryx fossil discovered in 1874 in Germany. It is the most complete specimen ever found, including a complete head.

Herculaneum was an ancient Roman town destroyed by the eruption of Mount Vesuvius in 79 A.D, along with Pompeii.

The title "Discourse on the Revolutionary Upheavals on the Surface of the Globe and On the Changes They Have Produced in the Animal Kingdom" is taken from an essay published by George Cuvier in 1825 on the theories of species extinction and catastrophism.

The Sin Nombre Virus, or the "nameless virus," is a hantavirus endemic in rodents and first found in the Four Corners Region of the United States.

The lines "If the weather should be warm, / be pleased to order the Bowels / to be taken out and some Pepper / put into the Body, but no salt / which would spoil the feathers" are taken from American naturalist Charles Wilson Peale's instructions to George Washington on how he should send the naturalist his dead pheasants.

The line "Do not touch the birds, they are covered in arsenic poison" is taken from a sign posted on Charles Willson Peale's displays at his Philadelphia Museum in the late eighteenth century, warning museum goers not to touch the preserved birds, as the birds were preserved using arsenic.

Leatherstocking, Trapper, Pathfinder, and Deerslayer are nicknames given to the main character Natty Bumppo by European settlers and Native Americans in *The Leatherstocking Tales* by James Fennimore Cooper.

A Naturalist in a Cannibal Land is a book written by British naturalist, insect, and bird collector A.S. Meek about his travels to New Guinea, Bougainville Island, and the Solomon Islands.

The lines "I have heard that when a crocodile / captures a calf or a human being, / it is usual for it to hide away the body / for some days before devouring it" are taken from A.S. Meek's book *A Naturalist in a Cannibal Land*.

Lord King God Bird and Pearly Bill are all common nicknames given to the Ivory-Billed Woodpecker, one of the largest species of woodpeckers once spread across the Southeastern United States and now considered extinct.

The lines "They sometimes cling to the bark / with their claws so firmly, as to remain / cramped to the spot for several hours / after death" are taken from John James Audubon's description of the Ivory-Billed Woodpecker in his book *Birds of America*.

Many of the lines in the poem "Specimen Days" are taken from the titles within Walt Whitman's prose work, *Specimen Days*.

"Laxarus Taxa" refers to an animal or plant which disappears from the fossil record, presumably because it is extinct, and then reappears.

Sir Richard Owen was an English biologist, comparative anatomist, and palaeontologist who coined the word "Dinosauria."

The lines "I regret very much the loss of this head, / it is impossible to save those that are taken / out of the water, and it is in the water or / Mires the Most entire bones are found" are taken from William Clark's correspondence to Thomas Jefferson during the Clark-Jefferson expedition of 1807 to recover complete Mastodon skeletons in Big Bone Lick, Kentucky.

The Viviparous Quadrapeds of North America is an illustrated scientific text co-authored by John James Audubon and Reverend John Bachman on mammals in North America, published between 1845 and 1854.

ACKNOWLEDGMENTS

MANY THANKS to *Horse Less Press* for publishing a selection of these poems in the chapbook *Terrible + Powerful + Wondrous.*

THANK YOU also to the editors of the following publications in which the poems in this book have been published, sometimes in earlier versions and with different titles: *Western Humanities Review, Guernica, Harp & Altar, Sink Review, NOÖ Journal, Ilk, Horse Less Review, Colorado Review,* and *Coconut Books* broadsides.

THANK YOU to following people for their friendship, support, and inspiration, without whom this book would not be possible: Eric Amling, Jesse Ball, Steve Cicala, Kate Colby, Bruce Covey, Cynthia Cruz, Ngoc Doan, Farrah Field, Joseph Massey, Kevin Prufer, Mark Rudman, Brenda Shaughnessy, Craig Teicher—and of course, Jen Tynes and Michael Sikkema at *Horse Less Press,* and Tony Frazer and everyone at *Shearsman Books.*

SPECIAL THANKS to Beth Steidle, not only for her friendship, support, and inspiration, but also for her work in beautifully designing this book. Thank you as well to artist George Boorujy, who so generously allowed us the use of his artwork for the cover.

To Ryan Murphy: Thank you for always believing in this book, and thank you for the love: *sweetbitter unmanageable creature who steals in.*

A NOTE ON THE TYPE

BULMER is a transitional serif typeface originally designed by William Martin (who also worked for John Baskerville) in 1792 for the Shakespeare Press. The types were used for printing the Boydell Shakespeare folio edition.

BELL (sometimes known as *John Bell*) is a serif typeface designed in 1788 by Richard Austin. An early example of the Scotch Roman style that had a short initial period of popularity, the face fell into disuse until it was revived in the 1930s.

www.ingramcontent.com/pod-product-compliance
Lightning Source LLC
Chambersburg PA
CBHW020216090426

42734CB00008B/1095